PICTURE FEATURE: ANTI-SCAMMING

Nathan Coppedge

PICTURE FEATURE:

How to Avoid Real Scams and Become Master of Your Business

BY NATHAN COPPEDGE

Nathan Coppedge

CONTENTS

Nathan Coppedge

I. INTRODUCTION

As an old person you would be expected to avoid scams, even if it was unfair or very difficult.

The same expectation put on old people exists for everyone. Unless you are confronted with one or two scams, meanwhile taking responsibility for the resources that are yours, then you won't stand a chance when old age rolls around.

Old age really sets the minimum guide for scam avoidance.

If we're sharp now, we might be sharp later, and some of the time that is all we know.

Nathan Coppedge

II. RECOGNITION

When scams happen (or better yet, when you *think* they happen), it is helpful to have wide-screen vision, like you're at a big-screen movie. You want to see clear blue skies. Clouds are the *very* worst thing, when it comes to scams.

Clouds might obscure the whole screen, destroying your sense of vision.

If you see a few clouds, this may sound contradictory, but you need to do some surveillance there, and this involves testing them by flying through them.

But, as you would know if you were a fighter pilot, being on alert means being in a state of the utmost readiness. You need to make sure your radar is on, and that you're prepared to turn around if you run into real trouble.

Remember, even if you turn around, you'll still have perspec-tive---you'll still have the big screen.

What you have to look out for are the clouds.

If you're ready---really ready and able--- you can fly through them.

But not if they fill up the whole screen!

III. AVOIDING THE RISK

No emergency trips to Africa or India unless you're a public health agency.

Don't be fooled by strangers that talk about passports and lottery winnings and the like.

Remember that no one is re-quired to be your friend. Even a long-time pal might miss you at the airport.

Trust your family, because they're your built-in defense against the outer world.

Trust those who think like you do---they are less likely to have a misunderstanding.

But remember the wide-screen vision: don't get stuck with peo-ple who are narrow-minded.

And, don't get doped by sophis-ticates who smoke cigarettes or who think everything comes at a price.

Friendship with those people often leads to disaster sooner or later, depending on who they are.

If you're in trouble, seek wise council, but remember even wise people sometimes have limited commitments.

If you want to survive alone in the jungle of life, remember, everything is learned from the wise, but the wise keep few friends.

More often than not, those who seem wise but have friends are those who suddenly pass away.

Perhaps wisdom does not keep well with those who have too many commitments.

These people have no trouble justifying their own deaths.

IV. SEEING CLEARLY

We've discussed the basics of the fighter plane analogy.

Now, let's discuss some of the features of the plane.

You want to look for good deals when your life is imperiled in the clouds!

You want to avoid blinding lights and religious testimony. Mere opinions are not enough to sway your pocket book. These might be brigands in disguise!

Remember, glare can cause the pilot to black out!

So, what are you looking for?

Four Things:

1. Consistency
2. Reasonable Commitment
3. Respectability
4. Nothing unreasonable

Remember: mere words don't make a difference by themselves. Any risk you take needs to be weighed against what you really stand to gain.

If there's no way to make a gain, then there's no reason to give in to manipulation, either.

Consider your background resources as an alternative to giving in.

Other notes:

1. Inconsistency is dangerous or shows unprofessionalism. Therefore, it is always to be avoided, except as a weak sign of respectability.

2. Reasonable commitment is about you and them, but it isn't always about making a deal. Make sure you more than understand everything you're getting into, if getting in is even an option at all.

3. Respectability is an important point in decision-making, because it allows you to judge whether other factors are falling into place. Is the person acting at his or her level of education, or a little too smart, or just not polished enough? These kinds of factors can give a tip-off about your level of commitment to what may seem like lies, or inform you of the difficulty of excessive demands.

Nathan Coppedge

V. USE YOUR INTUITION

Are you generally lucky?

Have you ever made a big risk that paid off?

Be realistic.

Nathan Coppedge

Nathan Coppedge

PICTURE FEATURE: ANTI-SCAMMING

Nathan Coppedge

BIO

Nathan Coppedge has been quoted in Book Forum and the Hartford Courant, and is a member of the International Honor Society for philosophy. He is the author of over thirty books.